SandCastle

Word Families Set 2

-ent as in cent

Pam Scheunemann

Consulting Editor Monica Marx, M.A./Reading Specialist

ABDO Publishing Company

Published by SandCastle™, an imprint of ABDO Publishing Company, 4940 Viking Drive, Edina, Minnesota 55435.

Printed in the United States.

Credits
Edited by: Pam Price
Curriculum Coordinator: Nancy Tuminelly
Cover and Interior Design and Production: Mighty Media
Photo Credits: BananaStock Ltd., Brand X Pictures, Corbis Images, Eyewire Images, Hemera, PhotoDisc, Rubberball Productions, Stockbyte

Library of Congress Cataloging-in-Publication Data

Scheunemann, Pam, 1955-
    -Ent as in cent / Pam Scheunemann.
        p. cm. -- (Word families. Set II)
    Summary: Introduces, in brief text and illustrations, the use of the letter combination "ent" in such words as "cent," "invent," "went," and "accent."
    ISBN 1-59197-233-7
    1. Readers (Primary) [1. Vocabulary. 2. Reading.] I. Title. II. Series.

PE1119 .S435145 2003
428.1--dc21   2002038620

SandCastle™ books are created by a professional team of educators, reading specialists, and content developers around five essential components that include phonemic awareness, phonics, vocabulary, text comprehension, and fluency. All books are written, reviewed, and leveled for guided reading, early intervention reading, and Accelerated Reader® programs and designed for use in shared, guided, and independent reading and writing activities to support a balanced approach to literacy instruction.

Let Us Know

After reading the book, SandCastle would like you to tell us your stories about reading. What is your favorite page? Was there something hard that you needed help with? Share the ups and downs of learning to read. We want to hear from you! To get posted on the ABDO Publishing Company Web site, send us e-mail at:

sandcastle@abdopub.com

SandCastle Level: Beginning

3 2872 00310 4415

-ent Words

bent

cent

dent

gent

scent

vent

Tess kept her head
bent.

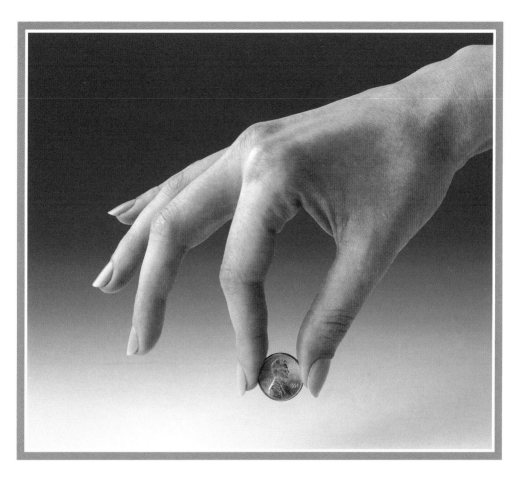

A penny is one cent.

The mailbox has a big
dent.

A man is sometimes
called a gent.

The flowers have a nice scent.

Mom cleans the vent.

Mr. Bob's Tent

Mr. Bob
was a gent.

Mr. Bob saw
a house
for rent.

FOR RENT

13

But poor Mr. Bob
didn't have a cent.

So his friend Rob lent
him a tent.

Mr. Bob took the tent
and away he went.

He set up the tent
by trees with good scent.

18

He put a vent
in the tent
to let in the scent.

Mr. Bob bent
to fit in the tent.

It was a night
very well spent!

The -ent Word Family

accent	lent
bent	rent
cement	scent
cent	spent
dent	tent
event	vent
gent	went
invent	

Glossary

Some of the words in this list may have more than one meaning. The meaning listed here reflects the way the word is used in the book.

bent   past tense of bend; to stoop or lean over

cent   a unit of money

dent   a pushed-in area on an item, usually made by force

scent   a pleasant smell

tent   a portable shelter made with nylon or canvas stretched over poles

vent   an opening that permits the escape of fumes or smoke

About SandCastle™

A professional team of educators, reading specialists, and content developers created the SandCastle™ series to support young readers as they develop reading skills and strategies and increase their general knowledge. The SandCastle™ series has four levels that correspond to early literacy development in young children. The levels are provided to help teachers and parents select the appropriate books for young readers.

Emerging Readers
(no flags)

Beginning Readers
(1 flag)

Transitional Readers
(2 flags)

Fluent Readers
(3 flags)

These levels are meant only as a guide. All levels are subject to change.

To see a complete list of SandCastle™ books and other nonfiction titles from ABDO Publishing Company, visit **www.abdopub.com** or contact us at:

4940 Viking Drive, Edina, Minnesota 55435 • 1-800-800-1312 • fax: 1-952-831-1632